Who Was
Jules Verne?

Who Was
Jules Verne?

by James Buckley Jr.

illustrated by Gregory Copeland

Penguin Workshop

To Conor, who is off on an adventure
of his own—JB

PENGUIN WORKSHOP
An Imprint of Penguin Random House LLC, New York

Text copyright © 2016 by James Buckley Jr. Illustrations copyright © 2016 by Penguin Random House LLC. All rights reserved. Published by Penguin Workshop, an imprint of Penguin Random House LLC, New York. PENGUIN and PENGUIN WORKSHOP are trademarks of Penguin Books Ltd. WHO HQ & Design is a registered trademark of Penguin Random House LLC. Printed in the USA.

Visit us online at www.penguinrandomhouse.com.

Library of Congress Control Number: 2016011722

ISBN 9780448488509   10 9 8 7 6

Contents

Who Was Jules Verne?

Jules Verne had longed to travel his whole life. He had grown up in eastern France, on an island in a river that led to the Atlantic Ocean. He had loved the ships that stopped regularly at the river port. As a boy, he had marveled at their tall masts and had been amazed at the cargo they carried into France: cocoa, spices, sugar, and exotic fruit such as mangoes.

By the time he was thirty-one, Jules had written poetry, plays, and magazine articles. But he wanted to write a book. He dreamed of writing an adventure story that would excite readers about the world around them.

He had read about some of the amazing places the world had to offer. He had read about British castles and the mysterious Scottish Highlands. He had read novels about knights and princes. He had also read books by Charles Dickens that described life in England. Now he was finally going to see those places in person. In the summer of 1859, Jules and a friend set sail from France to the islands of the United Kingdom.

The pair sailed on a cargo ship called the *Hamburg*. As the ship cut through the cold waters of the Atlantic, Jules was overjoyed. He stayed up at night to look at the stars. By day, he stood at the rail and watched the ocean ahead for signs of land. After the two friends arrived in Liverpool, England, they took a train to Scotland. There Jules was stunned by the high mountains, the huge rolling valleys, and the misty lakes. Jules saw the mystical Northern Lights—waves of colored lights visible in certain places north of the Equator—and went deep into mines in the hills.

On the way home, they also visited the famous city of London.

After he returned to France, Jules knew what he wanted to write about. Within a year, he had started work on the adventure novels that would make him one of the world's most popular authors. The young boy who had marveled at the ships bringing the world to him grew up to be a writer who took readers around the globe on a series of marvelous adventures.

CHAPTER 1
The Boy Who Loved Ships

Jules Verne was born on February 8, 1828, in Nantes, France. Almost as soon as he could walk, he was ready to travel.

The Verne family home was located on Feydeau Island, which is in the middle of the Loire River. The island is part of the city of Nantes.

After about a year, the Vernes moved into the part of the city that was on the mainland, where Jules's brother, Paul, was born in 1829. Their father, Pierre, was a successful lawyer. The family had a nice home with room for the two maids who helped their mother, Sophie.

The Vernes lived on the second floor of the building, because the first floor often flooded when the river rose above its banks. From the balconies in their home, Jules and Paul watched the boats move up and down the river. Nantes was where many ships from around the world arrived in France.

A shop not far from Jules's home sold birds and animals from far-off lands. At night, Jules could sometimes hear the cries of parrots and monkeys from the shop.

As a young boy, Jules wanted more than anything to see the places those ships had come from. He later wrote, "In my imagination, I climbed their shrouds [ropes], I scrambled to their topmasts, I gripped the knobs of their masts.

How I longed to cross from the quayside [shoreline] and tread their decks!" But Jules's father had other plans for his firstborn son. He wanted Jules to become a lawyer, too.

When Jules was six, he and Paul were sent to a boarding school to begin their education. Although the school was not far from their home, the boys lived at the school. The brothers learned to read, write, and solve math problems.

But when they could, they ventured into the fields. Jules later wrote that he and Paul would climb tall trees and rest in the branches. "We chatted, read, and hatched plans to travel, while the branches [were] shaken by the wind."

When Jules was nine, Pierre rented a vacation cottage for the family in a village farther east along the river. While there, Jules and Paul finally learned to sail. They borrowed a small boat and put it into the shallow river. They were soon able to steer the boat, sail it with the wind, and begin to live out the adventures they dreamed of . . . even though they always returned home in time for dinner.

The following year, in the summer of 1838,
Jules was sailing alone on the boat and ran into
some trouble. A part of the bottom of the boat
broke, and the little ship sank! Jules scrambled to a
nearby sandbank. Surviving this small shipwreck,
he felt like a castaway. He wrote later that he
thought of making a hut or creating a fishing

line to catch food. This happened in one of his favorite books, *Robinson Crusoe*. But the tide went out quickly, and Jules easily waded through the shallow water to the safety of the shore.

The Verne family eventually included three daughters as well: Anna, Mathilde, and Marie. With five children, Pierre and Sophie needed more room. In 1840, they moved to a new and larger apartment. Pierre had become very rich. The family could now afford beautiful furniture, a large clock over the mantel, and even separate rooms for the maids.

Castaways

The term *castaway* usually refers to a survivor of a shipwreck. The two most popular castaway stories of all time are *Robinson Crusoe* and *The Swiss Family Robinson*.

Robinson Crusoe was written by Daniel Defoe and published in 1719. It was based on the real-life adventure of a Scottish sailor named Alexander Selkirk. He had been stranded on an island and lived alone for many months. Defoe's castaway, Crusoe, is alone at first, but

later finds a native person he calls Friday.

In 1812, Swiss author Johann David Wyss's book *The Swiss Family Robinson was* published. In that novel, a family with four sons is shipwrecked while on a journey to Australia. They are forced to live for a long time on an island in the Pacific.

Late in his life, Jules Verne wrote a sequel to the Wyss story. In 1900, his book *The Castaways of the Flag* was published, describing new adventures for the Robinson family.

Jules and Paul started at a new school. At St. Donatien, they studied Latin, Greek, and poetry.

Jules found that he didn't like school much, but he did like writing. He wrote poetry and short stories, and he read as much as he could. As he read and wrote, Jules began to think that perhaps the life of a lawyer was not for him.

CHAPTER 2
Away to Paris

Jules graduated from high school in 1846. He and Paul both wanted to leave home and join a ship's crew. Paul soon began training as a marine cadet. Pierre insisted, however, that Jules become a lawyer. Jules was disappointed, but did as his father asked. He left home to study for his law-school exams in Paris.

Jules loved Paris. He loved the bustling streets filled with people from around the world. He loved the big buildings, the carriages that jammed the broad avenues, and the theaters that showcased plays and music.

In August 1848, he passed his tests and became a lawyer. Jules moved into a small apartment with his friend Edouard Bonamy. Neither man had much money, but they enjoyed living in the middle of the city. Jules's family sent him a little money.

His landlady brought him meals. Though he was not living the comfortable life anymore, Jules was very happy. He spent his free time writing plays, poems, sonnets, and songs.

Was his father happy about that?

No!

Pierre did not think his son should waste his time writing. Few writers of this time could hope to earn a living. Very few people read anything other than newspapers, and books sometimes sold only a handful of copies. Magazines did not pay writers very much. Pierre did not want his son to waste his education. He also wanted him to come home some day and take over the law firm.

But Jules kept writing. In an 1848 letter, he wrote,

"It's fantastic . . . to be in close touch with literature, to sense the direction it's going."

In Paris, Jules had the chance to meet many other writers.

Through his uncle, Jules was introduced to Victor Hugo, one of the most famous French writers of all time. He also became friends with Alexandre Dumas. Young Alexandre introduced him to people in the publishing business. "We became chums almost at once," Jules later wrote. "I may say he was my first protector."

Victor Hugo

Alexandre helped Jules with his story ideas. One of them became the first play written by Jules to be performed onstage. In 1850, *Broken Straws* ran for two weeks in Paris. The play was about a

The Dumas: Father and Son

Alexandre Dumas (1802–1870) was one of the most popular writers in France in the 1800s. He began his career writing plays and then novels. His most famous work was *The Three Musketeers*, about soldiers working for the king of France. He also wrote *The Count of Monte Cristo*, about the fall and rise of a French aristocrat.

Dumas's son, also named Alexandre (1824–1895), also became a well-known author. His most famous novel was *Camille*. In French, the writers are often called Dumas *pére* (say: PEAR) and Dumas *fils* (say: FEES), father and son.

member of the royal family. Jules was overjoyed, but when he sent his father the news, Pierre was very upset. He still worried that his son would never succeed as a writer.

In 1851, Jules sold his first magazine story. Another story appeared soon after. It was called "A Balloon Journey." Airplanes would not be invented for another fifty years. Hot-air balloons were the only way people knew how to "fly" at the time. In the story, a balloon trip turns dangerous when a criminal tries to stop the heroes. With this story, Jules's own journey as a writer was just beginning.

Hot-Air Balloons

In 1783, the Montgolfier brothers of France inflated a huge cloth bag with hot air. Their bag—sometimes called the envelope, but actually the balloon itself—was attached to a wicker basket the men could ride in. Because heated air rises, so did their balloon. It was the first manned balloon flight.

Over the next century, balloonists experimented with hot-air and gas-filled balloons, taking longer and longer trips. The balloons went wherever the wind blew. Passengers could only control how the balloon went up and down. People on the ground were often thrilled to see the enormous colorful floating objects.

Today, it is much easier to control hot-air balloons. They are still used for gathering scientific data, pleasure trips, and even advertising.

By 1852, Jules's father had had enough. He said he would stop sending money to help him. Pierre even offered to give his own business to Jules, if he would come home and work as a lawyer. Jules did not accept. Though he had his law degree, Jules never did work as a lawyer. Instead, he followed his dream to become a writer.

To do that, he took just about any writing job he could. He spent time with Alexandre Dumas and his other writer friends. In 1852, he

began work at the Lyric Theater as a secretary. For two years, he created posters, kept track of the theater's budget, and helped choose the plays. Finally, Jules had a steady job that enabled him to pay his own bills.

In 1856, Jules attended the wedding of an old college friend. There he met Honorine-Anna-Hebee de Viane Morel. Jules wanted to marry Honorine. But without a good job, he would not be able to convince her family that he was worthy of Honorine. So he began to work as a clerk to businessmen who traded stocks. It was not a writing job, but it paid his bills. In January 1857, Jules and Honorine were married.

She brought a dowry, which is money a woman gives her husband as a gift when they marry. Honorine's dowry let the family live comfortably. Honorine was a widow and had two young daughters, Valentine and Suzanne. So Jules was now a husband and a stepfather.

Even while working in the stock market, Jules kept writing. He published long articles about art, biographies of famous artists, and plays about life in Paris.

In 1859, Jules was lucky enough to take his first sea voyage. He and his friend Aristide Hignard went to England and Scotland.

Aristide's brother worked for a cargo shipping line. He offered the pair a free trip. In Scotland, Jules saw some of the places he had only read about in books. Jules was thrilled and inspired by what he experienced. His lifelong love of adventure, no longer just a daydream, was now becoming real.

Life in Paris was nothing compared to riding the waves on a big ship, taking long hikes through craggy mountain ranges, or exploring ancient castles in the Scottish Highlands.

When he returned, Jules was full of new ideas.

CHAPTER 3
Finally, a Novelist

In 1861, Jules and Honorine had their first child. They named the baby boy Michel.

A year later, Jules met the man who would change his life forever. Pierre-Jules Hetzel was a magazine and book publisher. He had worked with many of France's most famous authors, including Victor Hugo, Émile Zola, and Georges Sand. Jules gave Hetzel

Pierre-Jules Hetzel

the manuscript for his longest story yet. Hetzel requested a few changes, which Jules happily

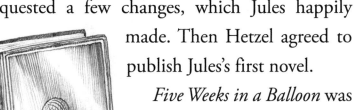

made. Then Hetzel agreed to publish Jules's first novel.

Five Weeks in a Balloon was published in early 1863. It told the story of a dramatic air journey over Africa.

Jules had never been in a hot-air balloon himself. But he was excited by the idea of it. Later he wrote that his book was not really meant to be about traveling by balloon. "I wrote *Five Weeks in a Balloon* not as a story about ballooning, but as a story about Africa. I always was greatly interested in geography and travel. There was no [way] of taking my travelers through Africa other than in a balloon."

Jules had read a lot about Africa before writing his book. He combined his skill at writing thrilling adventures with new discoveries in science that were happening in the world. This was a totally new way of writing fiction.

Five Weeks in a Balloon did not sell well at first. But later that year, the balloonist Nadar launched an enormous balloon called *Le Géant* (The Giant). Nadar was a friend of Jules. They belonged to a group of men who gathered to discuss the latest science news.

Nadar was also a photographer and was one of the first people to take aerial photographs—from high above the ground in his balloon. The flight of the *Géant* inspired people to buy Jules's book. At this time, all around Jules—in Europe and far away in America—many new ideas were coming to life. Scientists and engineers were making discoveries that changed the way people lived. Engines that used steam power were designed to make ships and trains travel faster than ever.

Men were experimenting with gliders and flying machines. Explorers were bringing back news from deep in the African jungle, the mountains of Asia, and many uncharted areas of the globe.

Jules seemed to be in the right place at the right time. He created a new kind of story, one that combined fantastic storytelling with real-life scientific developments. Though Jules never used the term "science fiction" to describe his writing, that is exactly what he was creating.

Hetzel believed that Jules's interest in science and his talent at developing adventure stories could be profitable for both men. He signed him to a contract promising to publish at least one of Jules's books every year.

What Is Science Fiction?

Science fiction, sometimes called "sci-fi," is a type of storytelling that blends scientific fact with things that come strictly from the writer's imagination. Science-fiction writers adapt ideas from technology, biology, engineering, and other areas. They wonder how scientific facts might be adapted in the future—or even how they might change the way people live. Science fiction is often about the possibilities of what *could be*: time travel, space travel, life on other planets, or artificial intelligence (computers).

Each book would be published chapter by chapter in a magazine. New chapters were printed every two weeks. When the story was over, the chapters were combined and printed as a single book. This is called serial writing. By having a new part of the story in each issue of his magazine, Hetzel knew readers would be impatient to find out what was happening in the story and eager to buy the next magazine.

In 1864, Jules wrote a long article in a French magazine about the author Edgar Allan Poe's work. Poe's tales of mystery and horror had influenced Jules's own writing.

The next serial adventure Jules wrote for Hetzel was called *The Adventures of Captain Hatteras.*

It is about a dangerous sea voyage. When Captain Hatteras and his crew finally reach the North Pole, they find a huge volcano erupting there. The story's first installment was published in Hetzel's magazine in 1864.

While he was writing, Jules continued to work as a business clerk. He and Honorine, along with their three children, moved into a larger home in a nicer part of Paris.

Edgar Allan Poe (1809–1849)

The American poet, editor, and author Edgar Allan
Poe lived only a short time, but his work had a major

impact on the writers of his time, as well as those who came after him. Poe was among the first writers to create mystery and horror stories. His dark imagination opened up new worlds for authors to explore.

Poe's most famous works were poems, such as *The Raven*, and short stories including "The Murders in the Rue Morgue," "The Tell-Tale Heart," and "The Gold-Bug." Today, he is regarded as the father of American mystery writing. The Mystery Writers of America have named their highest honor after him: the Edgar Award.

That summer, Jules returned to Nantes. Now that he was a published author, with the promise of much more work to come, he was welcomed home. Neighbors came by to greet the writer, whom they had known when he was a boy. They threw parties to welcome Jules and his family.

While in Nantes, Jules worked on his next novel, called *Journey to the Center of the Earth.* The story is about a scientist named Professor Lidenbrock who believes that volcanoes in Iceland provide a path to the Earth's core. He travels with his nephew and a guide into caves that  lead them far underground. There they discover a river that takes them on a long raft journey. After finding ancient fossils and evidence of huge human beings, they make it back to the surface by coming out of a volcanic eruption . . . in Italy!

Journey to the Center of the Earth was so popular that a larger illustrated version was published in 1865, with two additional chapters.

The novel once again showcased Jules's interest in exploration and new scientific discoveries. And his readers were just as excited by the thrilling possibilities as he was. A magazine review of *The Adventures of Captain Hatteras* showed that people understood what he was doing. "It is difficult to mix fiction and science without weighting down the one or diminishing [making less] the other. Here they enhance each other in a happy union."

His last two novels had made Jules one of the most famous writers in France.

CHAPTER 4
The Extraordinary Journeys

After his stories about the North Pole and the middle of the Earth, Jules sent his next characters on an even more surprising adventure. In *From*

the Earth to the Moon, a group of former soldiers plan to use one of their largest cannons to launch a missile to the moon. A man named Michel Ardan offers to travel in the missile and to explore the moon himself. Ardan makes it into orbit just as the story ends. Jules had named Ardan in honor of his good friend Nadar.

"Ardan" is an anagram of the name Nadar. The first chapters of *From the Earth to the Moon* were published in the fall of 1865, and the book was out for sale in time for Christmas.

Four Details about the Future that Jules Verne Got Right

In *From the Earth to the Moon*, and its sequel, *Around the Moon*, Jules Verne seemed to foretell some of the actual details of spaceflight to the moon, which did not happen until 1969—more than one hundred years later!

• The men in the book used Florida as their launch point. The spot they chose was not far from where NASA's Apollo missions blasted off in the 1960s.

• Three men rode in the novel's metal space capsule, just as real-life astronauts would do.

• The story's space travelers first tested their invention by sending up animals. In the early 1960s, monkeys and dogs were sent into space before humans.

- Both Jules's space travelers and the real-life astronauts landed back on Earth with a huge splash in the ocean.

Continuing their successful partnership, Hetzel and Jules signed a new contract in 1866. They agreed to publish three books a year. Hetzel called the new series of books The Extraordinary Journeys. About Jules he said, "His aim is to sum up all the geographical, geological, physical, and astronomical knowledge amassed by modern science, and to present the story of our universe."

Jules continued to read many types of scientific journals and to meet with as many experts as he could. He joined groups like the Circle of the Scientific Press to read about science news and hear lectures from famous scientists and inventors. He also gathered ideas for his stories by traveling around France and other parts of Europe. He took a summer trip—alone, or with friends and family—almost every year until the late 1880s.

In 1867, he planned a much longer trip.

He and Paul went to the United States, one of the few times Jules left Europe in his life. Together they sailed across the Atlantic Ocean on the *Great Eastern*, a massive steamship. Jules was so amazed by the ship that when they stopped in London,

he rowed all around it in a smaller boat so he could get a close look at every part of the huge steamer!

Arriving in New York, they stayed in a fancy hotel on Fifth Avenue. The hotel was the first in the city to have an elevator! Then the brothers traveled up the Hudson River to see the mighty Niagara Falls. Jules loved America. In many of his later books, he included American characters and US locations.

When he returned home with his notebooks full of ideas and observations, Jules found that the world of science and industry had come to *him*. The Universal Exposition of 1867 in Paris brought the wonders of the world right to his doorstep.

The Universal Exposition of 1867

From April 1 through October 31, 1867, the French government hosted a huge fair in Paris. It was called the Universal Exposition, and it showed off some of the newest scientific and engineering creations of the modern world. More than fifty thousand exhibits—including one for the brand-new form of energy, electricity—were displayed by countries from around the world.

Vue Générale de l'Exposition universeille de 1867

One of the highlights of the Exposition was the Gallery of Machines. It was designed by Gustave Eiffel, who later designed and built the Eiffel Tower. Visitors to the Gallery, which was the size of a football field, could see the first mechanical submarine and other underwater craft.

As many as fifteen million people visited the Universal Exposition.

CHAPTER 5
Captain Nemo

A lifelong love of the sea helped Jules write the novel that made him more famous than ever. He called it an idea "that perfectly fits the subject." Jules wanted to combine all the things that he was really passionate about, including rotors and flying machines. He researched machinery and read about sea voyages.

Jules was so excited about this new book that he wrote to Hetzel, "if I don't pull this book off, I'll be inconsolable." *Inconsolable* means so sad that there is no way to make you feel better.

Twenty Thousand Leagues Under the Sea tells the story of Captain Nemo, a mysterious man who commands the mighty submarine *Nautilus*.

The twenty thousand leagues in the title refers to the distance traveled (about sixty thousand miles), not the depths to which the submarine sank. (A league is an old measurement of about three miles. It originally indicated the distance a person could walk in one hour.)

At the Universal Exposition in Paris, an actual submarine called the *Nautilus* had been on display.

On Captain Nemo's *Nautilus*, the inside was not cramped, smelly, and dark as on real submarines. Instead, Jules Verne's *Nautilus* had large bedrooms for passengers. An onboard organ provided entertainment. There was a museum filled with paintings that Nemo had collected on his travels, along with natural wonders such as giant clams, tiny corals, and colorful starfish.

And Nemo's library had twelve thousand books. Electric light filled every room, and the mighty engines that drove the sub—which was more than 220 feet long—were also electric.

After taking on three passengers, Nemo goes on an around-the-world underwater adventure. The group travels under the ice cap of the North Pole, battles giant squid, explores the coral reef of the Red Sea, and even spots the transatlantic cable. After his passengers escape during a storm, Nemo and the *Nautilus* disappear in a huge whirlpool off the coast of Norway.

Jules took nearly three years to write *Twenty Thousand Leagues Under the Sea*. Hetzel decided to publish it in two separate volumes, six months apart. Jules delivered the first part of the novel before he had finished writing the story. This gave Hetzel the chance to ask for changes to make the second part better.

The year of steady research, writing, and fixing
details of his latest book was hard. Jules needed a
break. He felt he was finally ready to buy a larger
sailing ship. All he had had before was a small
fishing craft. He hired builders, and the work
began. "The boat is making progress," he wrote
in 1869. "She's going to be fantastic. I'm in love
with this assembly of nails and planks." When
it was finished, he named the boat *Saint-Michel*
after his young son.

Connecting Continents

In the 1830s, the telegraph was perfected by American Samuel Morse. The wires of the telegraph carried signals from place to place. This worked well on land. Telegraph poles were put up, and wires connected major cities and

Samuel Morse

towns. But was there a way to send telegraphs between continents?

Companies in America and England were set on doing this. Several attempts to lay the transatlantic cable were made from 1856 to 1867. It was difficult work. Often, the cables broke.

In 1866, a new cable was made and laid by the *Great Eastern*, a mighty steamship. On July 27, the first message was sent on this new transatlantic cable. The creation of the transatlantic cable was a huge step forward in world communications. It enabled messages to be sent in a matter of minutes—rather than weeks.

Coincidentally, Jules Verne took his only trip across the Atlantic Ocean on the *Great Eastern* a year later in 1867, during its first voyage after finishing its work laying the cables.

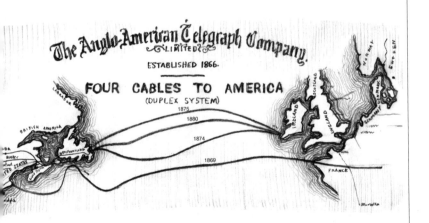

Together, the Vernes had many day-trip adventures from their summer home on the northeast coast of France. They were happy days filled with lots of family time and afternoons on the ocean. By 1870, the Vernes returned to Amiens, the city north of Paris where Honorine had grown up. She had wanted a larger house and more space than they could ever find in Paris. The success of Jules's writing had created a wonderful life for his family.

CHAPTER 6
A War and a Balloon

In August 1870, Jules went to Paris to receive the National Order of the Legion of Honor, France's highest award. He was now the most popular author in France. Things were going very well for Jules and his family, but that all changed in late 1870, and not just for the Vernes. War broke out between France and Prussia. Enemy forces invaded France and captured Paris.

Jules was too old to become a soldier, but the government did put him to work. They ordered Jules to use the *Saint-Michel* as a patrol boat. He sailed up and down the French coast for weeks. The crew never spotted any enemy ships, and Jules spent most of his time on his patrols writing.

The Franco-Prussian War

In 1870, Prussia was one of several independent states in the center of Europe. Its leader was Otto von Bismarck. He wanted to unify those states into a single nation, Germany. France was not happy about this plan, which they felt threatened their country. In the summer of 1870, the two countries went to war over this. The armies of Prussia and other German states proved too powerful. France fought for nearly a year, but had to surrender in 1871. Prince Otto became the chancellor of a new united German Empire. France remained a separate country.

When Jules finally did make it back to Paris to deliver manuscripts to his publishers, he found the offices closed. The fighting in the streets had made doing business impossible. Jules did not have an income and was forced to stay in Paris.

The war had made life difficult for everyone, even for France's most famous writer. For a time he became a clerk again to earn money. France's war troubles came to an end in the summer of 1871, but in November, Pierre Verne died. By then, Jules's father had become a great supporter of his son's work and was proud of all that he had accomplished.

Toward the end of 1871, Jules was working full time in Paris, but his wife and children were still living in Amiens. Hetzel finally began paying Jules again in early 1871. Soon after, Jules finished the book that would end his money worries forever.

Around the World in Eighty Days was published in the summer of 1872.

In the book, Englishman Phileas Fogg accepts a bet to travel around the entire world in eighty days. Today, that can take just a few days, but in 1872, many nations still did not have railroads, and of course, cars and airplanes had not yet been invented.

Phileas Fogg races through many countries, pursued by a British detective who wrongly believes that he is a bank robber. Phileas is joined by Passepartout, a French servant whose creativity and gymnastic skills help them escape several dangerous situations. On the way, they rescue a princess named Aouda in India, and she and Phileas fall in love.

The book has a twist ending. The trio arrives back in London certain that they are a day late, even after burning parts of their ship to provide fuel for the last dash to England. But they realize that they have actually *gained* a day by traveling east instead of west. They race to their meeting, and Fogg wins the bet.

The book was among the most popular Jules and Hetzel had ever published. As each new chapter of the serial was printed in the newspaper, the story was sent around the world, just as Phileas Fogg had been. In some countries, readers did not understand that the episodes were fiction, and so they began searching for Phileas themselves.

Jules enjoyed writing the book, perhaps as a way to cheer up after the sad days of the war. "If you could imagine how amused I am with my journey around the world in eighty days," he wrote to Hetzel. "I dream about it! Let's hope our readers are equally amused."

The book was turned into a stage play—also written by Jules. As the author, he made much more money from the play than he did from the book, enough to ensure a comfortable life for his family.

Nellie Bly

In 1889, an American journalist was inspired by *Around the World in Eighty Days*. She wanted to try to actually repeat the stunt by traveling around the world in just eighty days.

Elizabeth Cochran (1864–1922), who wrote under the name Nellie Bly, took only seventy-two days to complete the trip. Along the way, the groundbreaking reporter traveled by train, steamship, and horseback. At every stop, she relayed stories of her travels to her editor at the *New York World*. Newspaper readers around America followed her every move as she raced to beat Phileas Fogg's fictional record.

Early in her journey, she made one quick detour. She traveled to Amiens, France, to visit with the great author Jules Verne, whose story had sparked her 24,899-mile adventure.

CHAPTER 7
The End of the Adventure

The years following the success of *Around the World in Eighty Days* were filled with adventures for Jules and his family. Jules was in his mid-forties. He had plenty of money. Jules decided to build a new, larger yacht, the *Saint-Michel II,* in 1876, and then buy an even larger one the following year, the *Saint-Michel III*. He and Honorine built a grand house in Amiens. Jules spent many hours in his office on the fifth floor of the house, overlooking the city.

By this time Michel had grown into a young man who was often in trouble. He did not stay in school and could not seem to keep a job. Jules had to pay his son's debts. For many years, Jules struggled to help Michel.

Jules Verne's house in Amiens

In 1884, Jules and Paul visited Gibraltar at the southern tip of Spain to see the famous Barbary apes—the only wild monkeys living in Europe.

Then the brothers sailed across the Mediterranean Sea to Morocco and Tunisia, parts of North Africa that were then French colonies. Honorine joined them for the second part of their trip, in Italy and Greece.

Wherever they went, Jules was welcomed as a celebrity. In Rome, Jules and Honorine had an audience, or special meeting, with Pope Leo XIII. In Venice, Jules was saluted with fireworks and his name spelled out in lights on a hotel.

Jules continued to write, producing at least two novels a year for the next twenty years. All were part of the "Extraordinary Journeys" he published with Hetzel. They include *The Giant Raft*, *The Green Ray*, and *Clipper of the Clouds*.

When he wasn't writing, Jules took part in the town life of Amiens. He and Honorine threw popular parties for their friends and neighbors.

At one, they asked people to dress as characters from one of his books. At another, they dressed as restaurant owners, pretending to serve all the guests.

In 1886, Jules was shot in the leg by his nephew, Paul's son Gaston. He was badly hurt and, in fact, the bullet stayed in his leg for the rest of his life.

Just a week after the shooting, while Jules was still in great pain, he received some very sad news. His longtime publisher and friend, Pierre-Jules Hetzel, had died.

For several months, Jules kept his leg up in bed or on a chair. Eventually, he was able to walk, though with a cane. To keep busy, Jules ran for and won a seat on the town council of Amiens.

He worked to make sure that poor people in the city were cared for. He also helped establish a permanent circus in the town.

In 1888, Jules wrote his only children's book. In *Two Years' Holiday*, a group of children is shipwrecked on an island. They battle fierce animals and pirates. They build a kite so they can look for rescue ships. In the end, they are all taken off the island and brought to Australia.

Castaway Kids

When Jules Verne wrote most of his Extraordinary Journeys, they were intended to appeal to people of all ages. The magazine that they originally appeared in was for adults and children. Over the years, English translations of his stories often had changes that made them easier for children to read and enjoy.

Verne's book *Two Years' Holiday* was written specifically for children. It told the story of a group of schoolboys shipwrecked off the coast of New Zealand and their struggle to survive on Chairman Island.

One young reader of the book was William Golding (1911–1993). Golding grew up reading Jules Verne's stories of adventure. He became a schoolteacher and later an author himself. In 1954, he published *Lord of the Flies*. Like Verne's book, it was set on an island and told the story of a group of shipwrecked boys and their struggle to govern themselves. *Lord of the Flies* has become one of the most-read books for young people in the world.

In 1897, Jules returned to one of his early inspirations, Edgar Allan Poe. The American writer had written a novel that Jules felt could be continued. So Jules created a sort of sequel for Poe's *The Narrative of Arthur Gordon Pym of Nantucket.* Jules wrote other books that were set in Greece, Scotland, China, Canada, the Antarctic, and along the Amazon River. His love of adventure and exploration never faded.

Jules was in his seventies and world famous. Magazine writers from the United States and England visited his home in Amiens. In one interview, he described his writing habits. He said

that he wrote a "first rough copy in pencil, leaving a half-page margin for corrections." He then rewrote it all in ink, often changing sections several times. He refused to use a typewriter, which had become common by the 1880s. Finally, after the manuscripts had gone to his publisher and had been set into pages (called *proofs*), he made even more corrections. "I consider that my real labor begins with my first set of proofs, for I not only correct something in every sentence, but I rewrite whole chapters."

By this time, Jules once again became close with Michel. His son had finally married and was doing some writing of his own.

Jules himself tried to keep writing as the twentieth century began. His wounded leg still bothered him, and his eyesight began to fail, too.

His hands were cramped from spending a lifetime writing by hand. When he was seventy-seven, he had a stroke and never recovered. Jules Verne's great adventure ended with his death on March 24, 1905.

CHAPTER 8
An Inspiring Life

For more than a decade after Jules Verne's death, Michel Verne continued to publish his father's work. Some of the stories were finished before Jules died. Some, however, were not. Michel completed them on his own.

This was not discovered until many years later. Readers did not know that the final books "written" by Jules Verne were the work of the two Vernes, father and son, together.

During his lifetime, Jules Verne wrote and published hundreds of novels, plays, poems, and magazine articles. New editions of his work have been published ever since. Eventually, his novels were translated into more than 140 languages. Some experts say he is the most translated author of all time.

Ray Bradbury

The great science-fiction author Ray Bradbury said, "we are all, in one way or another, the children of Jules Verne." Since Jules's death, many authors have taken readers to the far corners of the galaxy and the universe, back in time, and into imagined futures, all by using the latest scientific discoveries and theories as inspiration. Jules thought of his writing as simply adventure stories, but because he based his work in scientific fact, he is often called "the father of science fiction."

Many of his stories have been turned into movies, TV shows, and comic books. *Twenty Thousand Leagues Under the Sea* was first made into a movie in 1916. This was at just the beginning of the film industry. And it was no surprise that Hollywood turned to the famous tales of Jules Verne for inspiration. A 1954 version of *Twenty Thousand Leagues Under the Sea* in full color proved to be even more popular. The 1956 movie version of *Around the*

World in 80 Days was a huge hit and won the Academy Award for Best Picture. It was remade in 2004 starring Jackie Chan as Passepartout.

Jackie Chan

Adventurers and explorers were inspired by Jules and his work. They took ideas from his stories and dared to make them come true. Admiral Richard Byrd flew an airplane over the North Pole in 1926 and said, "Jules Verne guides me."

Submarine pioneers such as William Beebe pointed to Captain Nemo as their inspiration. The rocket scientists Werner von Braun and Robert Goddard read Jules's books when they were children. Famous astronomer Edward Hubble was a Jules Verne fan. And on the far side of the moon, a rock formation has been named the Jules Verne crater.

Nearly ninety years after his death, another book by Jules was published. He had written it in 1863, very early in his writing career. Pierre-Jules Hetzel had refused to publish it, so Jules Verne had put it aside. The book was called *Paris in the Twentieth Century*. It became a best seller in 1994.

In the book, Jules looked ahead to what his beloved city of Paris might be like in the future. Amazingly, he predicted the huge impact that cars would have on our society, the widespread use of elevators, the invention of fax machines, and trains that would run on magnets.

Throughout his life, Jules Verne looked to the horizon, first as a child learning to sail and later as a writer. As he wrote, he imagined all the wonderful possibilities the future might hold, and he did his best to make them come true in the pages of his extraordinary journeys.

JULES VERNE

Timeline of Jules Verne's Life

1828	Jules Verne is born on February 28 in Nantes, France
1848	Moves to Paris to live year-round
1850	Sees first play, *Broken Straws*, produced
1852	Works as a secretary at the Lyric Theater
1857	Marries Honorine Morel
1859	Takes first trip at sea, to the United Kingdom
1861	Son Michel born
1863	Publishes first novel, *Five Weeks in a Balloon*
1864	Publishes *Journey to the Center of the Earth*
1865	Publishes *From the Earth to the Moon*
1869	Finishes writing *Twenty Thousand Leagues Under the Sea*
1870	Called to serve as a ship captain in the Franco-Prussian War
	Named to the French Legion of Honor
1872	Publishes *Around the World in Eighty Days*
1886	Shot in the leg by his nephew Gaston
1888	Elected to town council of Amiens, France
1905	Dies on March 24, 1905, in Amiens, France
1994	Final novel, *Paris in the Twentieth Century,* is published

Timeline of the World

1825	—	Nicholas I becomes tsar of Russia
	—	The first modern railway opens in England
1848	—	In France, a revolution ousts King Louis-Philippe
1853	—	Russia and England begin to fight in the Crimean War
1859	—	Charles Darwin publishes the revolutionary biology book *On the Origin of Species*
1861	—	American Civil War starts and lasts until 1865
1863	—	The Football Association, the first organized soccer group, forms in England
1869	—	The Suez Canal, linking the Mediterranean and Red Seas, opens
1871	—	Franco-Prussian War ends with a united Germany and France's Napoleon III out of power
1876	—	Alexander Graham Bell invents the telephone
1883	—	The Indonesian volcanic island of Krakatoa explodes, killing more than thirty-six thousand people
1885	—	Karl Benz of Germany puts a gasoline engine into a three-wheeled cart, creating what some call the first automobile
1886	—	The complete Statue of Liberty is unveiled in New York Harbor, a gift from France to the United States
1901	—	Italian inventor Guglielmo Marconi sends the first radio message across the Atlantic Ocean
1903	—	Wilbur and Orville Wright are the first to successfully fly an airplane

Bibliography

* Books for young readers

Butcher, William. *Jules Verne: The Definitive Biography*. New York: Thunder's Mouth Press, 2006.

Lottman, Herbert R. *Jules Verne: An Exploratory Biography*. New York: St. Martin's Press, 1996.

*Schoell, William. *Remarkable Journeys: The Story of Jules Verne*. Greensboro, NC: Morgan Reynolds, 2002.

Verne, Jules, and R. H. Sherard. *Jules Verne: His Own Account of His Life and Work*. A. J. Cornell Publications, 2012. E-book.

Verne, Jules. *Jules Verne Collection*. Doma Publishing, 2012. E-book.